Original title:
Joyful Growth

Author: Thor Castlebury
ISBN HARDBACK: 978-9916-88-172-9
ISBN PAPERBACK: 978-9916-88-173-6

The Journey to Bright Horizons

With every step beneath the sky,
We wander forth, our spirits high.
The path is long, yet hearts ignite,
In search of dreams that shine so bright.

Through forests deep and mountains tall,
We hear the whispers of the call.
Each twist and turn, a tale unfolds,
Of courage strong and hearts of gold.

The river flows with stories old,
Of daring quests and friendships bold.
We lift our eyes, the stars align,
And in their glow, our hopes entwine.

As dusk gives way to dawn's embrace,
We find our strength, we quicken pace.
For every trial fuels our drive,
Together, yes, we will arrive.

Beyond the hills, the future waits,
A world anew, through shining gates.
With hope as our unwavering guide,
We march ahead, side by side.

Moments of Bright Expansion

In the dawn's gentle light, we rise,
With hope that dances in our eyes,
Each heartbeat a moment, pure and clear,
Embracing the warmth, shedding the fear.

Winds of change whisper so sweet,
Carrying dreams on fleetest feet,
Every breath a chance to ignite,
In moments of expansion, take flight.

A Garden of Cheerful Dreams

In the heart of spring, colors bloom,
Each petal whispers joy to consume,
A canvas of laughter, bright and bold,
Where stories of wonder silently unfold.

Breezes carry scents of pure delight,
In this garden of dreams, spirits ignite,
Children's laughter, the sweetest song,
In the embrace of cheer, we belong.

The Radiant Journey

With every step, the world shines bright,
Paths unfurling under soft twilight,
Stars awaken as shadows play,
Guiding our hearts along the way.

Mountains tall and valleys wide,
In radiant journeys, we abide,
Through trials and triumphs, spirits soar,
Each moment a treasure, we explore.

Sun-Kissed Transformations

Beneath the sun's warm embrace, we grow,
In the glow, hidden strengths start to show,
Each sunrise a promise, a brand new day,
Transforming the shadows, lighting the way.

Seasons whisper secrets to the trees,
In sun-kissed moments, we find our ease,
As colors shift, we learn to adapt,
In transformations, our souls enwrapped.

A Fable of Flourishing Souls

In shadows deep, the seeds do lie,
Awaiting warmth, beneath the sky.
With gentle hands, the earth they grace,
Their whispered dreams in time find place.

From silence blooms the tale of light,
As hearts emerge, dispelling night.
With every breath, their spirits rise,
Embracing life, they paint the skies.

Vibrant Voices of Renewal

In fields adorned with vibrant hues,
The call of spring, the old imbues.
Each petal sings, a tale reborn,
In harmony, the world is sworn.

Through every note, the joy resounds,
As life anew in colors bounds.
From gentle whispers to bold refrain,
The vibrant voices break the chain.

The Untamed Joy of Becoming

A river flows, wild and free,
In every twist, a mystery.
Through hidden paths, it learns to bend,
Embracing change, it finds no end.

In pushing forth from roots so deep,
The joy awakens, dreams to keep.
With each new dawn, the heart takes flight,
In untamed joy, we find our light.

A Garden Alive with Beat

In every corner, life will spark,
The garden dances, leaves the dark.
With rhythms flowing, petals sway,
A symphony of bright array.

The bees will hum, the birds will sing,
As life unfolds, embraces spring.
With every heartbeat, life holds sway,
In gardens lush, we dance and play.

Rebirth in the Quiet Moment

In silence whispers soft and low,
The seeds of change begin to grow.
With every breath, a chance anew,
The heart beats strong, the soul breaks through.

In twilight's hush, we find our grace,
Embracing light in shadowed space.
Among the stillness, dreams take flight,
A phoenix rising into the night.

The Alchemy of Blossoming

From earth's embrace, the buds will bloom,
In golden sun, dispelling gloom.
Each petal's touch, a story told,
In colors bright, like rays of gold.

The dance of life, a vivid spree,
A canvas rich with harmony.
In every fragrance, hope is spun,
With every blossom, we are one.

Reaching for the Sky

With arms outstretched, we greet the dawn,
As dreams like clouds begin to spawn.
The horizon calls—a vibrant plea,
To grasp the stars, to dare to be.

In every heartbeat lies a spark,
To challenge shadows, face the dark.
Together, we unlock the door,
And soar above forevermore.

Medley of Bright Beginnings

Each moment holds a tapestry bright,
Threads of hope in morning light.
With gentle hands, we weave our fate,
In the dance of love we celebrate.

The song of life, a sweet refrain,
In harmony, we break the chain.
With open hearts, we start anew,
In every end, a chance to view.

Seeds of Hope in the Dirt

Buried deep in the earth,
Little dreams wait to sprout.
Each one whispers of worth,
In silence, they shout.

Rain kisses the ground,
Nurturing soft, tender roots.
In darkness they're found,
Growing tall in their suits.

The sun brings the light,
Guiding shoots toward the sky.
From shadows to bright,
They reach with a sigh.

Hope dances in rows,
With colors that burst and shine.
From seeds, love still grows,
In the heart where they twine.

The Joy of Reaching Upward

Hands stretched high to the sky,
Reaching for dreams far and wide.
With each moment, we try,
To let our spirits glide.

Clouds whisper sweet tales,
Of journeys yet to unfold.
Through storms or through gales,
We rise with hearts bold.

The sun warms our faces,
As we climb to the peak.
No more hidden places,
Our voices grow strong, not weak.

In the dance of the trees,
We find joy in the climb.
With every soft breeze,
We cherish the rhyme.

Sunrise Over the Blooming Fields

Morning breaks with a glow,
Sunlight spills on the land.
Colors burst, life in tow,
Nature's brush in hand.

Petals open wide,
Greeting the warmth of the day.
With beauty as their guide,
They wave in bright array.

Butterflies take to flight,
Dancing in the golden rays.
In this pure delight,
We lose track of the days.

Fields bask in the sun,
Together, vibrant and free.
In unison, we've won,
A joy for all to see.

Lush Promises of Tomorrow

Whispers of the breeze,
Carry secrets of the night.
With hope, our hearts seize,
And dreams take wondrous flight.

In gardens of the mind,
Future blooms, wild and bright.
With each goal, we find,
Steps towards the light.

Days painted in gold,
Every moment we embrace.
Stories yet untold,
Await in time and space.

With love as our guide,
We journey through the years.
In laughter, we abide,
While chasing away fears.

A Kaleidoscope of Possibilities

In the dance of light, they weave,
Colors merge, hearts believe.
Shifting shades in vibrant play,
Dreams unfold in bright array.

Every twist reveals a hue,
Endless paths, all fresh and new.
Infinite choices, wonder's call,
A vivid world, for one and all.

Within the glass, reflections spark,
Endless journeys from a mark.
Life's mosaic, pieces blend,
In every turn, beginnings bend.

Each moment holds a hidden art,
Kaleidoscope of life, pure heart.
The beauty lies in every chance,
A spectrum bright, a joyful dance.

Colors of the Heart in Bloom

Petals open, soft and shy,
Whispers of love dance and sigh.
Hues of passion, blush of grace,
In each heartbeat, find your place.

Sunlit gardens, vibrant dreams,
Rays of hope in gentle streams.
Crimson roses, golden sun,
In every color, life's begun.

Azure skies and emerald leaves,
Nature sings, the spirit believes.
From every shade, a story told,
In heart's embrace, treasures unfold.

Unity found in myriad tones,
Love's palette where beauty roams.
Every bloom, a fleeting start,
Colors of the soul, pure art.

Tides of Transformation

Waves crash softly on the shore,
Each ebb carries dreams to explore.
With every tide, new shapes arise,
Transformation whispers, never disguise.

Through the currents, we are drawn,
To the rhythm of dusk and dawn.
Life renews in fleeting flow,
In the depths, our true selves grow.

Silvery moons guide the night,
Embrace the change, let it ignite.
Drifting sands, a testament,
To the paths where hearts are bent.

From the depths, we find our way,
Winds of change shelter the stray.
Tides of life, forever swirl,
In their embrace, we rise and unfurl.

Indomitable Spirit of Growth

In the cracks of concrete, seeds find,
A spirit fierce, resilient kind.
Against the odds, they seek the sky,
With every struggle, learn to fly.

Raindrops fall, nurture the dream,
From the darkest storms comes a beam.
Roots dig deep, spread wide and strong,
In the heart of struggle, we belong.

Mountains high, valleys below,
Through the challenges, we learn to grow.
Each scar a story, every fight,
An indomitable will, shining bright.

In every sunrise, rise anew,
Hope's embrace in every view.
From the ashes, we find our way,
Indomitable spirit, come what may.

Boundless Horizons

Beyond the hills, where skies are wide,
Dreams of adventure gather and glide.
Waves of whispers call out in awe,
Opening hearts to the great unknown.

With each step taken, the spirit will soar,
Chasing the sunlight forevermore.
Through valleys deep and mountains tall,
The horizon beckons, inviting us all.

The Dance of Flourishing Souls

In twilight's glow, we begin to sway,
Echoes of laughter drift in the bay.
Together we twirl, in rhythm we find,
The beauty of life, entwined and aligned.

Like petals of flowers in soft spring rain,
Every heartbeat whispers, joy to remain.
Bound by the music, our spirits ignite,
Dancing through shadows, embracing the light.

Nature's Embrace of Happiness

Beneath the boughs, where the wildflowers bloom,
Nature's sweet fragrance dispels all gloom.
Gentle streams babble, caressing the stones,
Whispering secrets to tree-clad thrones.

In the warmth of sunbeams, laughter takes flight,
Birds sing their stories, a pure delight.
Along winding paths, joy may unfold,
In nature's embrace, our dreams can be told.

Varieties of Bliss

In moments of silence, joy's whispers reside,
In the heart of a child, where wonders collide.
Through laughter and tears, we find our way,
Each flavor of bliss colors our day.

From sun-kissed mornings to starlit nights,
Each heartbeat reminds us of life's simple sights.
In friendships and love, the essence is clear,
Varieties of bliss symphonize here.

Hues of Happiness in the Breeze

Soft whispers dance in the air,
Colors twirl without a care.
Sunshine paints the skies so bright,
Joyful hearts take flight tonight.

Gentle laughter fills the space,
Each moment, a warm embrace.
Fluttering leaves join the play,
Chasing worries far away.

In the fields where dreams are sown,
Every seed of hope has grown.
Life's canvas, vivid and wide,
In this bliss, we shall abide.

Melodies of the Unfolding

Notes cascade like drops of rain,
Symphonies that break the chain.
In the hush of twilight's glow,
Music whispers soft and low.

Time unwinds, a gentle stream,
Every chord, a related dream.
Harmonies call from the deep,
Awakening the soul from sleep.

In this dance, the heart feels free,
To the rhythm of infinity.
Each heartbeat plays a sacred part,
In the symphony of the heart.

Navigating the Path of Becoming

Steps of courage mark the way,
With each dawn, we find our say.
Winding trails and hidden doors,
Open minds, the spirit soars.

Lessons learned from every fall,
Rise again, we heed the call.
Hurdles crossed, we find the grace,
In the journey, we embrace.

Echoes guide with truths to share,
Dreams ignite the fervent care.
Every choice, a spark of light,
In this voyage, futures bright.

The Heartfelt Rise

From the valley, voices lift,
Hopeful hearts, a precious gift.
Together in the morning's glow,
We unite, and courage grows.

In the struggle, strength we find,
Casting shadows far behind.
Hands held firm, we stand as one,
Facing fears, the battle won.

With each heartbeat, dreams ascend,
Every moment, we transcend.
In this rise, our spirits soar,
Boundless love forevermore.

Buds of Laughter

In gardens where the children play,
Laughter echoes, bright and gay.
Buds of joy begin to sprout,
Filling hearts with cheer throughout.

A soft breeze whispers through the trees,
Floating joy like petals, free.
In every giggle, in every smile,
Life blooms brighter for a while.

Moments shared, a treasure's worth,
In sacred space upon this earth.
With each chuckle, we find grace,
In laughter's warm, embracing space.

So let the buds of laughter grow,
In hearts where love and kindness flow.
For every giggle, every cheer,
Creates a world that's bright and clear.

Radiance Unfurled

In quiet dawn, the sunlight spills,
Over hills and gentle rills.
Awakening dreams, a soft embrace,
Casting warmth on every face.

The flowers stretch, their colors bold,
A tapestry of stories told.
Each petal gleams in morning's light,
A dance of hues, pure and bright.

With every ray that pierces through,
A promise whispers, fresh as dew.
Nature sings a song so pure,
In radiance, our hearts are sure.

So let us bask in this rich glow,
As moments blossom, softly flow.
In every heartbeat, let love swirl,
Embracing life, radiance unfurled.

The Blooming Heart

In shadows deep where hope would hide,
A bloom emerges, full of pride.
Its petals soft, of vibrant hue,
A silent vow, forever true.

With roots that dig into the past,
It nurtures dreams, a love built to last.
Through storms that rage and winds that howl,
The heart stands strong, it won't throw in the towel.

In every struggle, it finds its way,
Turning darkness into day.
For in the soil of tender care,
The blooming heart learns how to dare.

So let it flourish, rise and shine,
This garden filled with love divine.
In every beat, in every start,
There lies the strength of the blooming heart.

Dancing in the Sunlight

Beneath the sky so vast and wide,
We twirl and spin, hearts full of pride.
With every step, our worries fade,
In sunshine's glow, our fears betrayed.

The trees stand tall, a joyous sight,
Their leaves alive, embracing light.
We move to rhythms, the world in tune,
Dancing beneath the bright, warm moon.

With laughter shared and spirits high,
We chase the clouds, we kiss the sky.
In every twirl, in every cheer,
We find the magic, pure and clear.

So let us dance, oh, let us play,
In sunlight's glow, we'll find our way.
With open hearts and steps so free,
Dancing in the sun, just you and me.

A Celebration of All That Blooms

In the morning's gentle light,
Petals unfurl with pure delight,
Colors dance, a vibrant show,
Whispers of spring, soft and slow.

A chorus of bees, busy and bright,
Buzzing with joy, taking flight,
Nature's perfume fills the air,
A symphony of love laid bare.

Each bud and leaf, a story sung,
From the earth, their song is wrung,
In every garden, life resounds,
A tapestry where hope abounds.

With every bloom, the heart takes wing,
In perfect harmony, we sing,
A celebration, wild and free,
Of all that grows, for you and me.

Woven Dreams in the Soil

In the depths where roots entwine,
Silent prayers in dark align,
Seeds of promise gently sown,
Whispers of growth remain unknown.

Beneath the surface, dreams take flight,
Stretching towards the golden light,
Tendrils reach, a quest for air,
Woven dreams that linger there.

Each leaf a canvas, each branch a tale,
Nature's stories, strong and frail,
From tiny sprouts to mighty trees,
Life's designs carried on the breeze.

In the soil, where wonders hide,
Life's adventures quietly bide,
With patience, nature finds her way,
In woven dreams of each new day.

A Chorus of Flourishing Lives

In meadows wide, where wildflowers bloom,
A chorus rises, dispelling gloom,
Bees hum softly, their sweet refrain,
Life's creation in joy unchained.

From towering trees to grasses low,
Every creature shares the flow,
A dance of light, a vibrant throng,
Nature's anthem, bold and strong.

In streams that whisper, in skies that gleam,
Life's mutual support is a common dream,
Together we flourish, intertwined,
A bond unbroken, ever aligned.

As seasons change, the song remains,
In every joy, in all the pains,
A chorus echoing through the air,
Celebrating life, forever rare.

Nature's Radiant Rebirth

With winter's chill now fading fast,
Nature awakens, free at last,
Golden sunbeams kiss the ground,
In this warmth, new life is found.

The crocus peeks from under snow,
Heralds of spring in radiant glow,
Trees don buds, a vibrant spree,
Nature's canvas, freshly free.

Rivers flow with playful cheer,
Life returns, we draw it near,
Butterflies float on gentle breeze,
A time to bloom, a time to seize.

In every heart, the spark ignites,
With nature's song, our spirit lights,
In radiant rebirth, we rejoice,
Together, we sing, united voice.

Whispers of Spring's Promise

Buds bloom softly in the light,
Birds return, taking flight.
Gentle rains kiss the ground,
Echoing life all around.

Colors burst in joyful sway,
New beginnings lead the way.
Sweet scents dance in the air,
Nature whispers, tender care.

Dewdrops glisten on the leaves,
Morning sun, the heart retrieves.
Hope arises from the frost,
In the warmth, no moment lost.

Colors of Dawn's Embrace

Golden rays paint the sky,
Shadows retreat, the night goodbye.
Nature wakes with a gentle sigh,
In the quiet, dreams still lie.

Peach and lavender swirl and blend,
Each hue a message, each note a blend.
Birds sing out, the world anew,
In dawn's embrace, life comes through.

Mist drapes softly on the hills,
Whispers of morning, joy that thrills.
As warmth unfolds, the day will start,
Colors of dawn speak to the heart.

Flourish in the Breeze

The trees sway with gentle grace,
Leaves whisper secrets, a soft embrace.
Petals dance in a playful spin,
In every gust, new life begins.

Flowers bloom, a vibrant sweep,
Filling gardens, memories to keep.
Honeybees hum, collecting bliss,
Nature's harmony, a sweet kiss.

Sunshine spills, a golden stream,
Life awakens from a dream.
In the breeze, we find our ease,
Flourishing moments, hearts appease.

Lively Roots Awakening

Beneath the soil, life begins,
Roots stretch out, embracing wins.
Awakening from winter's sleep,
Whispers of growth in silence deep.

Small sprouts push through the earth,
Announcing spring, a time of birth.
With tender hope, they reach for grace,
Life unfolds in every space.

Each green shoot finds its way,
Shivering leaves where dawn holds sway.
In this dance, we're intertwined,
Lively roots, our fates aligned.

Whispers of the Awakening Earth

Beneath the roots, a tale unfolds,
Soft murmurs rise from the ancient molds.
Life stirs gently in the morning light,
Nature's secrets, hidden from sight.

The breeze carries echoes of new birth,
Awakening dreams, a promise of mirth.
Grasses dance softly with every sigh,
Whispers of life beneath the vast sky.

Mossy blankets hug the stones so tight,
Crickets sing proudly, welcoming night.
Each droplet of dew reflects a gleam,
A world reborn, vibrant with the dream.

With every heartbeat, the earth awakes,
A symphony played by the gentle lakes.
Roots intertwine, as if to embrace,
In perfect harmony, they find their place.

The Symphony of the Blooming Heart

Petals unfold in a radiant hue,
Each blossom whispers, 'I live for you.'
In gardens painted with colors bright,
The heart finds its strength in the light.

Butterflies dance on delicate wings,
The wind carries tales of the joy that it brings.
Every heartbeat matches the bloom,
A chorus of life in the springtime's room.

From soil to sky, the connection is real,
Nature's embrace is a love we can feel.
Each flower a note in a beautiful song,
Together they play, where we all belong.

With every fragrance, a memory stirs,
The symphony sings as the heart gently purrs.
In the vibrant tapestry woven with care,
We find our place in the fragrant air.

Sunlight Through the Canopy

Golden rays pierce the verdant leaves,
Creating patterns where sunlight weaves.
Shadows dance on the forest floor,
Nature's artistry, an endless encore.

Squirrels scurry with mischief and glee,
While sunlight bathes the roots of the tree.
Birds serenade the morning so bright,
Chirping in tune to the soft morning light.

Leaves rustle softly, a gentle choir,
Speaking of dreams and hearts that aspire.
Through branches entwined, the light filters down,
Adorning the earth with its luminous crown.

In this haven of green, we find our peace,
A place where worries and troubles cease.
Sunlight through canopy, a heavenly grace,
Wrapping the wilderness in warm embrace.

The Colors of Rebirth

In springtime's grasp, the world awakens,
With splashes of color, hope is unshaken.
Tulips and daisies join in the dance,
Each petal a chance, a beautiful chance.

Fields are adorned with a vibrant array,
Nature's palette brightens the day.
Pastels and bolds in a perfect blend,
A canvas of life that will never end.

With each brush stroke, the earth gets a say,
In shadows of winter, the colors display.
A rainbow of dreams upon the blue skies,
In the art of rebirth, true beauty lies.

As seasons shift, the colors will grow,
A cycle of life in a rhythmic flow.
Embrace every hue, let your heart sing,
For in every ending, new beginnings spring.

A Chorus of New Beginnings

With dawn's light breaking free,
A symphony starts to play,
Each note holds hope anew,
Singing dreams that sway.

The canvas awaits our brush,
Colors dance in the breeze,
Dreams woven with gentle touch,
Whispers shared with trees.

A seed planted in the earth,
Yearning for the sun's embrace,
Fingers crossed for rebirth,
In this sacred space.

Voices rise in unison,
Celebrate what's yet to come,
Together, we become one,
In this world, we hum.

The Art of Happy Harvests

Fields spread wide in golden hue,
Joy blooms in every space,
Hands that work know what to do,
With patience, time, and grace.

Gathering fruits of labor's toil,
Baskets filled to overflow,
The earth's bounty, rich and royal,
In each heartbeat, love will grow.

Laughter dances in the drops,
Underneath the azure sky,
Together, we will never stop,
As nature's gifts pass by.

With every smile, we will share,
The flavors of our days,
In gratitude, a heartfelt prayer,
Life's harvest, love displays.

Blossoms in the Sun

Petals open with the day,
Kissed by golden rays,
Nature sings a soft ballet,
In the warmth, it sways.

Colors burst in joy's refrain,
Filling hearts with cheer,
In the garden, love's domain,
Each blossom, bright and clear.

Bees hum softly as they weave,
Threads of life, bound tight,
With every bloom, we believe,
That shadows turn to light.

Embrace the moments as they come,
With each fragrance found,
Together beating like a drum,
In love, we are unbound.

A Tapestry of New Beginnings

Threads are woven, bright and bold,
In patterns rich and deep,
Each story waiting to be told,
In dreams we gently keep.

Stitch by stitch, we craft our fate,
With colors from our soul,
In the silence, we create,
A vision, a shared goal.

Together in this dance of life,
We find our unique song,
Each challenge, joy, and strife,
In unity, we belong.

New beginnings, fresh and bright,
With every dawn's first gleam,
In the beauty of the light,
We embrace a shared dream.

Tapestry of Laughter

In the garden where we roam,
Joy dances like the sun's warm glow.
With friends beside in laughter's dome,
Memories weave, a vibrant show.

Whispers float on breezy air,
Echoes of delight resound.
Each moment cherished, bold and rare,
In every smile, pure love is found.

Underneath the silver moon,
Stories shared in soft embrace.
Laughter's song, a sweet commune,
Together in our sacred space.

As twilight bleeds into the night,
Hearts entwined, we softly sway.
In this tapestry, pure delight,
Wrapped in joy, we laugh and play.

The Symphony of Blossoms

Colors burst beneath the sky,
Petals whispering in the breeze.
Nature's choir, a soft reply,
Harmony that puts hearts at ease.

Morning dew on vibrant hues,
Each bloom sings a song so sweet.
Gentle caresses, nature's muse,
Life's rhythm flows beneath our feet.

Budding dreams in every sprout,
Spreading love where shadows lay.
Together we shall dance about,
In this symphony, we sway.

As day progresses into night,
Stars awaken, blooms softly close.
In every heart, a spark of light,
The world, in peace, calmly doze.

Euphoria in Every Petal

Delicate petals unfold slow,
Whispers of joy fill the air.
Colors of life, a vibrant show,
In every bloom, love laid bare.

Sunlit mornings, soft and bright,
Each flower's grace tells a tale.
In their fragrance, pure delight,
Nature's magic will prevail.

With gentle hands, we touch the dream,
Harvesting moments, pure and true.
Euphoria flows, a sparkling stream,
In every petal, love shines through.

As twilight casts soft hues around,
Each blossom leaves its sweet embrace.
In memories, we joyously found,
The bittersweet, a tender grace.

Rise, Like Morning Glories

Awakened by the dawn's first light,
Morning glories reach for the sky.
In shades of blue, they bloom so bright,
Their beauty makes the heart comply.

Each petal sings of new beginnings,
As sunbeams gently warm the earth.
Life's fresh promises, soft and winning,
In every dawn, a newfound worth.

With every breeze, possibilities,
Embrace the hope in every sigh.
Together, we shall dance with ease,
With morning glories, we will fly.

As daylight wanes, the stars will gleam,
Yet still, their essence lingers near.
In every heart, we share a dream,
To rise each day without a fear.

New Horizons on the Wind

Beneath the vast and open sky,
A whisper calls me to the heights.
With every breath, I yearn to fly,
As dreams take flight on morning lights.

The waves of change begin to swell,
Casting shadows on the shore.
With courage, I will break the spell,
And seek the paths forevermore.

With every gust, new choices show,
Horizons shift, and futures gleam.
I follow where the wild winds blow,
Embracing life, my sacred dream.

In every heartbeat, hope ascends,
And every moment shapes the way.
Onward to journeys without ends,
New horizons beckon each day.

Echoes of a Lively Heart

In the stillness, joy awakes,
A melody of laughter flows.
With every beat, connection makes,
The rhythm only friendship knows.

Through vibrant colors, stories weave,
Each echo dances in the light.
In shared moments, hearts believe,
In every word, the pure delight.

With whispered dreams, we soar and glide,
Beneath the stars and moonlit glow.
Together, we walk side by side,
Embracing all that life can show.

These echoes linger, sweet and bright,
An anthem of the love we share.
In every day, in every night,
Our lively hearts, a bond so rare.

Dances of the Resilient Spirit

In shadows cast by trials faced,
The spirit sways, it bends, it breaks.
Yet in the depths, strength is embraced,
With every challenge, courage wakes.

Through stormy skies and restless seas,
The dance of life, a bold refrain.
With every step, the heart agrees,
Resilience blooms through all the pain.

With every twist, a story told,
In graceful movements, power shines.
The spirit's dance, both fierce and bold,
A testament to life's designs.

So let us twirl through trials grand,
Embrace the rhythm, let it flow.
In unity, together we stand,
Dancing onward, through ebb and glow.

Radiant Steps of Progress

With every step, a vision grows,
A path illuminated bright.
Each choice we make, a seed we sow,
In gardens filled with hope and light.

Through struggles faced, we rise anew,
With lessons learned and courage found.
In every heart, a fire will strew,
The way to dreams, where we are bound.

Like petals opening to the sun,
Our spirits soar on wings of grace.
In unity, we'll all be one,
Together, we shall find our place.

So let us tread on roads untold,
In step with visions yet to be.
With radiant hearts and spirits bold,
We forge the path to destiny.

Chasing the Light

In the morning glow we roam,
Where shadows dance, we find our home.
With every step the sun ignites,
We chase the dreams, embrace the heights.

Golden rays paint the skies,
Whispers of warmth, where hope replies.
Through fields of gold, hand in hand,
Together we rise, together we stand.

Moments flicker, like stars at night,
Fleeting seconds, pure delight.
We gather dreams, like fallen leaves,
In this wild world, our hearts believe.

As dusk descends and colors fade,
In twilight's grasp, our fears evade.
Chasing the light, we'll find our way,
In the silent whispers of the day.

Embracing the Unfolding

Petals open, a story told,
In nature's grace, the strong and bold.
With each new dawn, we learn to grow,
Embracing change, we ebb and flow.

In stillness found, a gentle sigh,
Dreams take flight, they dance and fly.
Here and now, we find our place,
In the woven threads of time and space.

The heart beats softly, passions rise,
With every breath, we're on the rise.
Unfurled wings in the sun's embrace,
We seek the beauty, we seek the grace.

As seasons shift and shadows pass,
In the unfolding, we find our class.
With open hearts, we navigate,
In the dance of life, we celebrate.

Sunkissed Whimsy

Beneath the sun's warm, golden glow,
We chase the breezes, let laughter flow.
In fields of daisies, dreams take flight,
Sunkissed whimsy, pure delight.

Butterflies flutter, colors ablaze,
In this moment, we lose our gaze.
Hand in hand, we skip and twirl,
In a world of magic, our hearts unfurl.

Splashing through puddles, splintered light,
Every drop is a pure delight.
Whispers of joy in every sound,
In this blissful state, we are unbound.

As day fades softly into night,
We hold our dreams close, hold them tight.
Sunkissed whimsy, forever bright,
In the canvas of life, pure and light.

Heartbeats in the Garden

In the garden where silence sings,
Heartbeats echo, life begins.
Petals blush with morning dew,
Nature's dance, so fresh, so new.

Beneath the arch of the ancient trees,
Whispers linger in the breeze.
Every bloom holds a story dear,
In the garden, love draws near.

Sunlight kisses the earth so warm,
In its embrace, we find our charm.
Through tangled vines, our spirits soar,
In heartbeats' rhythm, we dream for more.

As shadows lengthen, stars appear,
In the garden, we lose our fear.
Every moment, a precious gem,
In the heartbeat of nature, we find our hymn.

Blossoming Beneath the Stars

In the garden of the night,
Petals shine, an ethereal light.
Whispers dance on cool, soft air,
Hope and dreams woven with care.

Under the moon's gentle gaze,
Flowers bloom in a silvery haze.
Each bloom tells a story anew,
Of longing hearts and skies so blue.

Stars peek through branches so wide,
Nature's beauty, a cosmic guide.
In silence, the blossoms unfold,
Carrying secrets, stories untold.

Night wraps the world in soft lace,
Creating a magical space.
Blossoming dreams beneath the night,
In the stars, we find our light.

Sprigs of Delight

Tiny leaves in the morning sun,
Whispers of joy, life's easy run.
Dewdrops glisten on vibrant green,
Nature's palette, a blessed scene.

Soft breezes carry sweet perfume,
Every corner, a life in bloom.
Petals flutter like laughter bright,
In the garden, pure delight.

In the shade of an ancient tree,
Children's laughter, wild and free.
Every sprig a story to tell,
In the haven where dreams dwell.

With each step, a secret shared,
In this joy, the world is bared.
Sprigs of delight call hearts to play,
In nature's arms, we find our way.

Beyond the Horizon's Edge

Where the sky meets the endless sea,
Waves whisper secrets, wild and free.
Golden light spills over the crest,
Inviting hearts to seek their quest.

Distant lands await the brave,
With stories of hope and the paths they pave.
In the twilight, dreams take flight,
Beyond the horizon, into the night.

Each footstep forward, a leap of faith,
Chasing visions, the heart's wraith.
Together, we greet the unknown,
In the vastness, we find our own.

Uncharted futures lie in wait,
Under the starlit, wondrous fate.
Beyond the horizon's endless call,
Life's grand adventure beckons us all.

The Echoing Laughter of Nature

In the rustling leaves, a joyous sound,
Echoes of laughter swirl around.
Birds sing melodies crisp and clear,
Nature's symphony, always near.

Rippling streams with playful sighs,
Reflecting hues of changing skies.
Every whisper, a joyful cheer,
Moments cherished, held so dear.

Breezes carry stories untold,
In the arms of the wild, bold.
The mountains listen with gentle grace,
In nature's laughter, we find our place.

Fields of flowers dance in delight,
Painting the world with colors bright.
The echoing laughter of the earth,
A reminder of life's precious worth.

Outstretching with Radiance

In the dawn, the light breaks free,
Reaching hands toward the sky.
Colors dance in vibrant hue,
Nature's gift, a wondrous view.

Whispers soft, the breeze does bring,
Promises of the joy we cling.
Every petal, every leaf,
Shares a story, glimpse of grief.

In the garden, life awakes,
Birds on branches, sweet heartaches.
Sunlight spills on emerald ground,
In this beauty, we are found.

With open hearts, we shall embrace,
The warmth that time cannot erase.
Together we will stand and shine,
Outstretching arms, our paths align.

The Gentle Climb toward the Horizon

Footsteps tread on winding trails,
Toward horizons, hope prevails.
With each step, the spirit grows,
Through the valleys, gently flows.

Peaks above, a soft embrace,
Whispered strength in nature's grace.
Every stumble, every rise,
Shapes the path beneath our skies.

Clouds above, like dreams they drift,
Carrying hopes, a precious gift.
In the distance, light persists,
Guiding us through morning mists.

With patience, we shall roam and seek,
In the silence, find our speak.
The gentle climb, a cherished song,
Toward the horizon, we belong.

A Festival of New Life

Buds awaken from their sleep,
Gentle whispers, secrets keep.
Nature's canvas, fresh and bright,
Painting joy in colors light.

Sprouts of green on fertile ground,
Life rejoices, peace is found.
Underneath the vast blue skies,
A symphony of soft replies.

Butterflies in playful flight,
Dancing beams of pure delight.
In this gathering, hearts unite,
A festival of love's pure light.

Together we shall celebrate,
Every moment, small or great.
With open arms, we'll cherish now,
A cycle new, a vibrant vow.

The Art of Embracing Change

Leaves will fall, the seasons shift,
In the storm, new dreams may lift.
Every moment brings a chance,
To adapt and join the dance.

Shadows come, then sunlight beams,
Transforming all our silent dreams.
In the face of tides that wane,
We find beauty in the pain.

Roots hold strong, but branches sway,
In the breeze, we'll find our way.
Each transition, a chance to grow,
In the changing, love will flow.

With open hearts, we'll pave the road,
Together share this heavy load.
The art of change, our lives rearrange,
In every chapter, we embrace the strange.

Nestled in Nature's Caress

Beneath the trees, soft whispers sigh,
A gentle breeze, as time drifts by.
Nestled close, the world feels right,
Nature's arms, a warm invite.

Colors dance in sunlight's gleam,
Rippling waters, a quiet dream.
Amidst the leaves, life finds its way,
In nature's lap, we long to stay.

Wildflowers bloom, a vibrant hue,
The earth alive, refreshed and new.
In this haven, hearts find peace,
In nature's love, we are released.

So let us wander, hand in hand,
Through forest paths, o'er golden sand.
In nature's book, our stories blend,
With every step, the journey's mend.

Wings of Transformation

In shadows deep, a whisper grows,
A spark within, where courage flows.
From egg to sky, the journey starts,
With hope anew in trembling hearts.

Wings unfurl, in colors bright,
Soaring high, embracing light.
From struggles past, a tale unfolds,
In every flap, my spirit holds.

Through trials faced, the chrysalis breaks,
In moments lost, the soul awakes.
With every flap, the past takes flight,
A dance of change in boundless height.

So here I stand, in freedom's grace,
With dreams aloft, I find my pace.
Embrace the change, let old ways cease,
For in my wings, I've found my peace.

Flourishing in the Embrace of Light

In morning's glow, the world ignites,
Petals bloom, revealing sights.
Sunbeams dance on dewdrops clear,
In the warmth, I feel you near.

Every leaf, a story spun,
In nature's arms, all is one.
With every ray, the shadows flee,
In light's embrace, I'm truly free.

Roots dig deep in fertile ground,
In soft earth, life's magic found.
Fingers stretch to kiss the sky,
With every breath, I learn to fly.

So let me bask in this pure glow,
In every moment, let love flow.
Flourishing where hearts unite,
In harmony, we share the light.

The Magic of Becoming

In silence deep, a spark ignites,
Transforming dreams on starry nights.
With open hearts, the journey starts,
The magic lies in brave new parts.

From shadows cast, we step into,
The unknown path, the radiant view.
Through every twist, our spirits grow,
In every step, the winds will blow.

Embrace the change, let fears dissolve,
In every challenge, we evolve.
Through trial and error, we start to see,
The magic of who we're meant to be.

So take the leap, let courage soar,
In the dance of life, we find our core.
The magic waits in every turn,
In becoming whole, our spirits yearn.

A Journey Written in Petals

In the garden where dreams unfold,
Petals whisper stories untold.
Each color an echo of time,
Softly weaving a rhythm and rhyme.

Winds carry tales through the air,
Gently brushing our skin with care.
Scents of adventure, sweet and bright,
Guide our hearts through day and night.

Footprints of love in the dew,
Each moment a treasure, pure and true.
Stars twinkle in the evening sky,
Reminding us to always fly.

As petals drift, they pave the way,
To futures where hope finds its sway.
Together we'll wander, hand in hand,
Through this journey, so beautifully planned.

Canvas of Fresh Adventures

Blank pages await with bated breath,
Colorful dreams shout, defying death.
Brush strokes dance in vibrant delight,
Crafting tales in the soft moonlight.

Taking chances like birds on the wing,
Each moment a story, a song to sing.
Splashes of laughter, dashes of fear,
Every heartbeat loud and clear.

Through forests of wonder and mountains grand,
We paint our journey, hand in hand.
With each sunrise, new hues ignite,
Our souls awaken to endless light.

In the gallery of life, we find our place,
A masterpiece woven with love and grace.
Together we bloom, in the colors we share,
In this canvas where dreams fill the air.

Seeds of Happiness Bursting Forth

In the earth where the sunlight beams,
Seeds of joy sprout, chasing dreams.
With gentle rains and warm embrace,
They flourish, filling every space.

Tiny bursts of life appear,
Each one a spark, each one a cheer.
Roots entwined, they grow as one,
Celebrating life beneath the sun.

With every bud, new stories rise,
Under the soft kiss of azure skies.
Nature's chorus sings so sweet,
As happiness blooms in every heartbeat.

Together we nurture, together we sing,
In this garden of love, joy takes wing.
For each seed sown is a promise made,
A future of laughter, never to fade.

A Crown of Sunshine

Golden rays dance upon our face,
Warming hearts with a gentle grace.
Nature's gift, a crown divine,
Shines brightly, our spirits entwined.

Fields of daisies sway in delight,
Beneath the sky, so vast, so bright.
Each bloom a treasure of warmth and cheer,
Whispers of joy, always near.

In every sunset, a promise lies,
A warmth that fills the evening skies.
With each dawn, we rise anew,
In the crown of sunshine, forever true.

Together we bask, hand in hand,
Facing the world, ever so grand.
For love and light will always stay,
In our hearts, come what may.

Paths Paved with Petals

Soft whispers guide us near,
On paths paved with petals clear.
Nature's blush in morning light,
A tranquil scene, a pure delight.

Each step blooms with gentle grace,
Weaving memories in this place.
In harmony, our hearts entwine,
As colors merge, so sweet, divine.

A fragrant breeze, it drifts along,
Carrying whispers of our song.
With every turn, new blooms arise,
Revealing beauty in our eyes.

Together we shall tread and roam,
Creating paths that lead us home.
In nature's dress, we find our way,
On paths paved with love each day.

Embracing Change with Open Arms

The winds of change begin to blow,
Inviting us to let life flow.
With open arms, we greet the new,
As skies shift from gray to blue.

The past may linger, soft and sweet,
But in the present, we find our feet.
Embracing moments, bright and bold,
Unraveling stories yet untold.

In every shift, we find our way,
Transforming night into day.
With courage in our hearts we stand,
Writing life's book with steady hands.

So let the changes come with grace,
In every challenge, find a place.
Together we'll bloom, together we'll heal,
Embracing change, we'll learn to feel.

The Melody of Growing Strong

In every note, the heart takes flight,
A melody that feels so right.
Through trials faced, we rise and learn,
In every struggle, our spirits burn.

With whispering winds and songs of cheer,
We gather courage, cast off fear.
Each harmony guides us along,
Resonating with a powerful song.

Together we create a symphony,
In moments shared, we find unity.
A rhythm rooted deep within,
The essence of our journey's spin.

As we grow strong, we stand as one,
Beneath the embrace of the golden sun.
In every heartbeat, let love play,
In the melody, we find our way.

Life's Canvas Painted Bright

With every stroke, a tale unfolds,
On life's canvas, dreams are bold.
The colors splash, both warm and cool,
Creating magic, breaking rules.

Brushes dance in joyful glee,
A masterpiece of you and me.
In vivid hues, our stories blend,
A beautiful journey with no end.

From shadows dark, to light divine,
We paint our hopes, our hearts align.
In every layer, lessons learned,
A canvas bright, forever turned.

So let us paint with passion strong,
In life's gallery, we all belong.
With every choice, new shades ignite,
Life's canvas painted, pure delight.

Celebrating the Unfolding

In the morning light we gather,
To witness life anew,
Petals bloom in vibrant colors,
As dreams begin to break through.

With laughter echoing softly,
We dance upon the grass,
Each moment filled with wonder,
As time begins to pass.

Nature whispers in the breeze,
Promises of what will be,
Together we embrace the change,
In joyful harmony.

A celebration of the heart,
As each new leaf unfurls,
We find beauty in the journey,
In this vast and precious world.

Dreams Taking Root

In the quiet of the night,
Seeds of hopes are sown,
Whispers of tomorrow,
Into the earth are thrown.

With the dawn, they start to stir,
Life begins to unfold,
Gentle dreams take their form,
In colors brave and bold.

Through the rains and hopeful sun,
Their journey has begun,
Nurtured by our patience,
Until they greet the sun.

We watch as they grow stronger,
Reaching up for the skies,
A testament of courage,
In every leap that tries.

The Horizon's Embrace

As the sun meets the sea,
A canvas spreads wide,
Whispers of the horizon,
Where dreams and hopes collide.

With each wave's gentle kiss,
The future feels so near,
A promise in the distance,
As stars begin to appear.

Together we chase the twilight,
Hand in hand we roam,
In the embrace of the sunset,
We find our way back home.

With the night drawing closer,
We breathe in the refrain,
The horizon's sweet allure,
In both joy and in pain.

A Serenade of the Seasons

In spring's tender beginning,
Blossoms burst into view,
Sweet melodies of laughter,
Echoing skies of blue.

Summer's heat ignites the day,
With warmth upon the skin,
Fields alive with golden light,
Where the dance of life begins.

Autumn paints the landscape,
In hues of orange and brown,
The rustle of the leaves,
As they gently fall down.

Winter wraps the world in white,
A hush upon the ground,
In this serenade of seasons,
Life's beauty can be found.

Eager Sprouts of Delight

In gardens green, new shoots arise,
Sunlight dances, reaching skies.
Whispers of life in morning's glow,
Eager sprouts begin to grow.

Softly swaying with the breeze,
Nature's magic, aiming to please.
Colors burst in joyful cheer,
Delightful wonders drawing near.

Roots entwine beneath the earth,
Cradling dreams of hopeful birth.
Each petal tells a story sweet,
Eager sprouts, where life's heartbeat.

Together they embrace the day,
In their presence, shadows play.
Nature's tune, a vibrant song,
Eager sprouts, where hearts belong.

Celestial Growth

Under starlit skies, we find,
Seeds of dreams, both pure and kind.
Cosmic winds bring tales untold,
Celestial growth in hands to hold.

Roots extend to touch the stars,
Wishes carried over far.
In every leaf, a spark ignites,
Celestial truths shine through the nights.

From soil rich, to heavens wide,
Nature's wonders, our constant guide.
Silent whispers in the dark,
Celestial growth ignites a spark.

Branches reach for love and light,
Blooming through the darkest night.
With every breath, a chance to soar,
Celestial growth forever more.

A Canvas of Vibrant Melodies

In the meadow, colors play,
Nature's brush paints bright array.
Each petal sings, each note a tune,
A canvas bright beneath the moon.

Fluttering wings and drifting leaves,
Crafting stories that nature weaves.
With every breeze, a symphony,
A vibrant melody, wild and free.

From golden sun to twilight's hue,
The canvas shifts in every view.
Brushstrokes of laughter, joy, and grace,
Nature's art, a warm embrace.

In harmony, we dance along,
To the rhythm of life's sweet song.
A canvas alive with boundless cheer,
Vibrant melodies drawing near.

Serendipity in the Meadow

A hidden path through fields of gold,
Whispers of secrets yet untold.
Happiness blooms where chance aligns,
Serendipity in sweet designs.

Wildflowers swaying, light and free,
Dancing with joy just like me.
Every step, a gift of delight,
Serendipity, pure and bright.

Sunlight dapples through the trees,
Gentle breezes, the buzzing bees.
In the meadow, life unfolds,
Serendipity, a treasure bold.

Embrace the magic of the day,
Let every moment lead the way.
In nature's arms, our spirits soar,
Serendipity forevermore.

The Dance of the Sprouting Seed

In the quiet earth, a whisper grows,
A tiny sprout breaks free from its clothes.
With gentle sunlight as its guide,
It reaches upward, full of pride.

The rain whispers sweet, a tender song,
Encouraging roots to dig down strong.
With every petal that starts to unfurl,
Life's magic dances in a vibrant swirl.

Nature's rhythm, a joyful beat,
Tiny leaves sway, a graceful feat.
Each unfurling brings a new dear friend,
In a tapestry where dreams transcend.

Together, they sway, a sight so rare,
Celebrating life in the warming air.
The sprouting seed, vibrant and free,
Embraces the world, as it's meant to be.

Laughter Among the Leaves

Laughter dances in the rustling trees,
Whispers of joy carried by the breeze.
Golden sunlight filters through the green,
Creating shadows where dreams can be seen.

Every leaf holds a secret to tell,
In the laughter that rings like a bell.
The branches sway, a playful delight,
As nature rejoices in morning light.

Children run wild, with spirits so free,
Chasing shadows, laughing in glee.
The leaves respond with a rustling cheer,
As laughter and nature draw ever near.

In this haven where spirits unite,
The melody of joy feels just right.
Among the leaves, life finds its way,
In laughter's embrace, we wish to stay.

Radiance of the Rising Dawn

As the night gives way to the glowing morn,
New light awakens, the world reborn.
Gentle hues dance on the canvas sky,
Whispers of hope as the day draws nigh.

The sun peaks slowly, a fiery eye,
Kissing the earth with a warm goodbye.
Golden rays stretch, declaring their claim,
In the warmth of dawn, all life feels the same.

Birds chirp merrily, a joyful tune,
Under the gaze of the gracious moon.
Nature speaks softly, in colors untold,
Embracing the light as the day unfolds.

With each rise, a promise so clear,
Of new beginnings in the atmosphere.
The radiance of dawn, a gift we adore,
A reminder that life offers more.

A Garden of Dreams Unfurled

In the heart of the earth, seeds start to sigh,
Dreams buried deep, beneath the sky.
Colors ignite as the blossoms emerge,
A garden of dreams begins to surge.

Each petal unfurls in delicate grace,
Creating a haven, a sacred space.
Fragrant whispers float on the breeze,
As the flowers dance with the teasing leaves.

Bees hum a tune, busy at play,
Painting the air in a joyous display.
The sun shines bright on this vibrant land,
Where dreams grow wild by nature's hand.

In this retreat where hopes intertwine,
A sanctuary where all hearts align.
A garden of dreams, alive and unfurled,
With every bloom, a new story is twirled.

Milton Keynes UK
Ingram Content Group UK Ltd.
UKHW020936041024
449263UK00011B/563

9 789916 881736